Our Pattern of Prayer

(Devotional Messages on the Prayer Life of the Apostle Paul)

By Al Hughes

Table of Contents

Introduction

Paul was a man of prayer. The first thing said of Paul after he was saved, *"Behold, he prayeth"* (Acts 9:11).

There are over thirty specifically recorded prayers of Paul in the New Testament. There are no exact words of Paul's prayers in Acts—only **historical instances** of him praying (Acts 9:11; 16:18, 25; 20:36; 28:8).

The specific words of Paul's prayers begin in his epistles. These are prayers **inspired by Holy Spirit** and preserved for us in the Bible.

Why is it important to study the prayers of Paul? Paul is a **pattern** for us to follow (read 1 Corinthians 4:16; 11:1; 1 Timothy 1:16; Philippians 3:17; 4:9).

Paul's prayers are somewhat different from the prayers we often hear in public, or maybe even our own prayers?

I pray God will use these brief devotions of some of Paul's prayers to make your prayer life more effectual.

Al Hughes
Mesa, AZ
April, 2021

PAUL'S PRAYERS #1 (Romans 1:8-10)

A Pattern for Prayer

First, I thank my God through Jesus Christ for you all, that your faith is spoken of throughout the whole world. For God is my witness, whom I serve with my spirit in the gospel of his Son, that **without ceasing I make mention of you always** in my prayers; Making request, if by any means now at length I might **have a prosperous journey by the will of God** to come unto you. For I long to see you, that I may impart unto you some spiritual gift, to the end ye may be established (Romans 1:8-11).

PAUL'S PRAYER WAS...

1. **INITIATED** with thanksgiving (*"First, I thank my God..."*; Psalm 100:4 — *"Enter into his gates with thanksgiving..."*; Philippians 4:6; 1 Timothy 2:1).
   - **Prayer, with thanksgiving, should go hand-in-hand** (Colossians 4:2 — *"Continue in prayer, and watch in the same with thanksgiving"*).

- Our prayers should being by thanking God! Paul typically began his epistles with a prayer of thanksgiving: 1 Corinthians 1:4 — *I **thank** my God always on your behalf, for the grace of God which is given you by Jesus Christ;* Colossians 1:3 — *We give **thanks** to God and the Father of our Lord Jesus Christ, praying always for you,* 1 Thessalonians 1:2 — *We give **thanks** to God always for you all, making mention of you in our prayers;* Philemon 4 — *I **thank** my God, making mention of thee always in my prayers…*
  - ➡ Think of how many people and churches Paul prayed for.
  - ➡ Paul did not wait to receive "prayer requests" to pray for them.

The thanksgivings of Paul's prayers are, for the most part, quite different from what we give thanks for in our prayers. We thank God for material provisions… bodily health… deliverance from some physical calamity, etc. We may occasionally offer a word of thanks for someone's conversion to Christ. These things are all good, but fall short of Paul's pattern in prayer.

As D.A. Carson points out:

> But by and large, our thanksgiving seems to be tied rather tightly to our material well-being and comfort. The unvarnished truth is that what we most frequently give thanks for betrays what we most highly value.[1]

- ➡ A convicting thought! Think about what you most often give thanks for in your prayers.
- ➡ If our affections are set on things above, and not on things on the earth, (Colossians 3:1-2), our prayers should reflect it (Matthew 6:21).

2. **INCESSANT** in practice (*"...that WITHOUT CEASING I make mention of you ALWAYS in my prayers..."* cf. Romans 12:12; Philippians 1:3; 1 Thessalonians 5:17). Paul was not erratic, but faithful in his praying for others. Paul did not just talk about praying. He actually prayed!

- • Prayer has been referred to as **"the pulse of a Christian's life."** How

---

[1] D.A. Carson, *Praying With Paul,* Baker Academic, Grand Rapids, MI, 2014, p. 23.

strong is the spiritual pulse in your life?

3. **INTERCESSORY** in nature ("*...I make mention OF YOU in my prayers*" cf. Ephesians 1:16 — *Cease not to give thanks FOR YOU, making mention OF YOU in my prayers*).

The **highest form of prayer** is intercessory prayer (completely unselfish). We cannot do anything of greater benefit than to pray for fellow believers.

- It is Abraham praying for Lot in Sodom (Genesis 18:23-33).

- It is Moses praying for the children of Israel when God was about to destroy them (Exodus 32:31-32).

- It is Samuel praying for the nation Israel (1 Samuel 7:5; 12:19-23).

- It is Job praying for his three "friends" (Job 42:10).

- It is Jesus praying for Peter, that his faith would not fail when he was sifted (Luke 22:32).

- It is Paul praying for Israel to be saved (Romans 10:1).

4. **INVOKING** of traveling mercies (v. 10 –
"*…I might **have a prosperous journey**…*).
He was specific in his request. Paul
longed to see these believers (v. 11).

Why did Paul want to visit them? His
desire was that He might help establish
them (v. 11). Paul had an unselfish heart.
He was willing to be spent for the sake of
others. He basically wrote the same thing
to the church at Corinth. *"Behold, the third
time I am ready to come to you; and I will not
be burdensome to you: **for I seek not yours,
but you… And I will very gladly spend
and be spent for you**"* (2 Corinthians
12:14-15).

Queen Victoria asked General William
Booth, founder of the Salvation Army,
what she could do for him. Booth
answered, "Your Majesty, some people's
passion is money, and some people's
passion is fame, but my passion has been
men."[2] May this be true of me.

5. **INGRAINED** in the will of God (v. 10 –
"*…**by the will of God**…*"). Paul

---

[2] R. Kent Hughes, *Romans: Righteousness from Heaven.*

conditioned his prayers on the will of
God. 1 Corinthians 4:19 — *But I will come
to you shortly,* **if the Lord will**... 16:7 — *I
will not see you now by the way; but I trust to
tarry a while with you,* **if the Lord permit**...
(cf. James 5:15).

PAUL'S PRAYERS #2 (Romans 15:5-7)

A Prayer for Believers to "Get Along"

Now the God of patience and consolation grant you to be likeminded one toward another according to Christ Jesus: That ye may with one mind and one mouth glorify God, even the Father of our Lord Jesus Christ. Wherefore receive ye one another, as Christ also received us to the glory of God. (Romans 15:5-7)

Paul prayed for the church to "get along" with each other and live HARMONIOUSLY (*"to be likeminded on toward another… That ye may with ONE in mind and ONE mouth …"*).

The **context** of Paul's prayer is patience towards weaker believers (14:1-6; 15:1-3).

Paul is praying for unity in the body of Christ. Psalm 133:1, *"Behold, how good and how pleasant it is for brethren to dwell together in **unity**!"* Not in uniformity of *opinion*, but rather in a uniformity of *forbearance*.

- In Ephesians 4:2-3 Paul exhorted Christians to *"forbear one another in love endeavouring to keep the unity of the Spirit in the bond of peace."*

Forbearance means restraint and tolerance — to "put up" with each other's opinions.

There are several controversial issues among good Christians: Dress codes; Christmas trees; styles of music; dispensational divisions; Baptist polity (communion); etc. These are **non-essential issues** that have nothing to do with salvation. Therefore, we need to pray for patience and forbearance towards other believers who do not understand the same liberty that we enjoy in Christ.

- Colossians 3:13, *"Forbearing one another, and forgiving one another, if any man have a quarrel against any: **even as Christ forgave you, so also do ye.**"*

God is addressed as *"**the God of patience and consolation.**"* These two qualities are essential for getting along with each other: Harmony requires us to be **patient** and **consoling** (comforting) towards one another

"ACCORDING TO CHRIST JESUS." We should be just as patient and loving toward one another as Jesus is to us. If God receives men with their weaknesses, we should also.

When a church is unified, God is glorified. *"That ye may with one mind and one mouth **glorify God**..."* A united local church is a church that glorifies God. A divided church dishonors God (Galatians 5:15 — *"But if ye bite and devour one another, take heed that ye be not CONSUMED one of another."*)

In C. S. Lewis' book, "*The Screw Tape Letters*," he describes some of the tactics of the devil. Screw Tape (the devil) advises Wormwood, his demonic nephew, how to keep a human from the truth: Satan (Screw Tape) says, "The church is a fertile field IF you just keep them bickering over details, structure, organization, money, property, personal hurts, and misunderstandings..." This is one of one of Satan's most effective devices—Sowing discord among the brethren. And God hates it (Proverbs 6:16-19).

Paul's PRAYERS #3 (Romans 16:25-27)

A Prayer of Praise

The grace of our Lord Jesus Christ be with you. **Amen**… *The grace of our Lord Jesus Christ be with you all.* **Amen.** *Now to him that is of power to stablish you* **according** *to my gospel, and the preaching of Jesus Christ,* **according** *to the revelation of the mystery, which was kept secret since the world began, But now is made manifest, and by the scriptures of the prophets,* **according** *to the commandment of the everlasting God, made known to all nations for the obedience of faith: To God only wise, be glory through Jesus Christ for ever.* **Amen.** (Romans 16:25-27).

Paul closes his letter to the Romans with a prayer or DOXOLOGY (a prayer of praise to God).[3]

Prayers are often concluded with the word *"Amen." "Amen"* literally means "so

---

[3] *Webster:* "[Gr., praise, glory; to speak.] In Christian worship, a hymn in praise of the Almighty; a particular form of giving glory to God.). See Jude 25

be it" or "may it be so." There are FOUR *"Amens"* at the end of Romans (15:33; 16:20, 24, 27).

A prayer for three things:

#1-**FIRST**, Paul prays for a **GRANTING** of grace upon the saints (v. 24).

- Paul closed every one of his epistles with this request.[4]
- How we all need this bestowal of grace! Do you pray for God to grant grace on your brothers and sisters in Christ?

#2-**SECOND**, Paul prays for believers to be **GROUNDED** (or ESTABLISHED–To establish something means to stabilize.[5]).

God establishes you *"according to"* **three things** Paul mentions in this prayer: (Notice three occurrences of *"according to"*):

---

[4] 1 Corinthians 16:23; 2 Corinthians 13:14; Galatians 6:18; Ephesians 6:24; Philippians 4:23; Colossians 4:18; 1 Thessalonians 5:28; 2 Thessalonians 3:18; 1 Timothy 6:21; 2 Timothy 4:22; Titus 3:15; Philemon 25; Hebrews 13:25.

[5] Colossians 1:23, *"...continue in the faith **grounded and settled**, and be **not moved away** from the hope of the gospel..."* 2:7, *"...**Rooted and built up in him, and stablished in the faith**, as ye have been taught."*

1. First, we are established **according to Paul's gospel and preaching** (...*according to* [1] *my gospel, and* [2] *the preaching of Jesus Christ...*).
   - **Paul's gospel** (Romans 2:16; 16:25; 2 Timothy 2:8 cf. 1 Corinthians 15:1; Galatians 1:8-9; 2:2). *"My gospel"* is a peculiar designation of the gospel Paul preached as opposed to *"another gospel"* preached by false teachers (2 Corinthians 11:4).

   Paul called it *"my gospel"* because he was the leading propagator of it. It is the "good news" Paul received specifically by revelation from God (Galatians 1:11-12) and it includes the whole body of revelation given to Paul.
   - **Preaching** Christ (1 Corinthians 1:23; 2:2; 4:5; Colossians 1:28). You cannot get too much preaching of Christ!
     ➡ A grounding of these two things will fortify a believer's faith.
2. Secondly, we are *established **"according to the revelation of the mystery,** which was kept secret since the world began, But now is made manifest, and by the scriptures of the prophets..."*

A *"mystery"* in the Bible is a truth hidden in the Old Testament and revealed by God in the New Testament.

It is like when a new car model is introduced. The car itself is covered with a sheet or canvas. You can see the shape of it, but not the details. The designer knows what the car looks like, but the general public does not. When the sheet is removed, the complete car is revealed.

There are seven mysteries revealed to Paul (a study in itself). The specific mystery Paul was referring in our text to was **the mystery of the Body of Christ composed of both Jews and Gentiles** (cf. Ephesians 3:3-6).

➡ A grounding in this mystery will fortify a believer's faith.

3. Thirdly, we are established *"according to"* God's plan of salvation – "...*according to the commandment of the everlasting God, made known to all nations for the obedience of faith:"*

God *"made known to all nations"* that people must exercise faith for salvation. *"The obedience of faith"* is another way of saying a person is saved by obeying God's call to believe on Christ (see Romans 1:5; 10:16; 1 John 3:23).

Are YOU grounded in the plan of salvation by grace through faith?

#3- THIRD, Paul prays for God to be **GLORIFIED** (v. 27). A final *"Amen."* This should be the ultimate desire of every believer.

- God's unparalleled **wisdom** — *To God ONLY wise…"* (1 Tim. 1:17; Jude 25).
- God's unending **worship** — *"…be glory through Jesus Christ for ever."*

  Amen!

PAUL'S PRAYERS #4 (1 Corinthians 1:4-7)

A Prayer for a Carnal Church

I thank my God always on your behalf, for the grace of God which is given you by Jesus Christ; That in every thing ye are enriched by him, in all utterance, and in all knowledge; 6 Even as the testimony of Christ was confirmed in you: So that ye come behind in no gift; waiting for the coming of our Lord Jesus Christ: (1 Corinthians 1:4-7).

Consider WHO Paul is praying for!

1) The local church at Corinth (v. 2). Corinth was a very worldly city in Greece — Commercial, cosmopolitan, corrupt, and carnal.
   - Paul, with Aquila and Priscilla, worked a year and a half to establish a local church in Corinth (Acts 18:1-11).
2) It was a **problematic** church. The Corinthian church was filled with cliques… carnality… marital issues… law suits against fellow believers… doubts

about Paul's apostleship... disorders at the Lord's Supper... misuse of spiritual gifts, etc.

Paul's prayer teaches us three things about **how to pray for carnal believers**.

1. Paul's **APPRECIATION** for them in spite of their errors and carnality (v. 4).
   - Paul lead some of these people to Christ (1:14, 16).
   - Paul loved these believers (16:24).
2. Paul's **ADHERENCE** to praying in thanksgiving (v. 4).
   - Paul was always thankful for the grace of God given to them by the Lord Jesus Christ (v. 4).
3. Paul's **ADMIRATION** for God's blessings on this church (verses 5-7). In spite of their carnality, there were some good things about the Corinthians.
   1) Their enrichment in utterance and knowledge.
   2) Their testimony of Christ.
   3) Their abundance of spiritual gifts (spiritual gifts are no indication of spirituality).

4) Their attention to the coming of
   Christ.

SUMMATION: When we pray for each
other, let's begin by…

- Thanking God for their testimony. And…
- How God has blessed them with spiritual
  gifts. And…
- For their attentiveness to Christ's return.

PAUL'S PRAYERS #5 (2 Corinthians 12:7-10)

A "Thorny" Prayer

*And lest I should be exalted above measure through the abundance of the revelations, there was given to me **a thorn in the flesh**, the messenger of Satan to buffet me, lest I should be exalted above measure. **For this thing I besought the Lord thrice**, that it might depart from me. And he said unto me, My grace is sufficient for thee: for my strength is made perfect in weakness. Most gladly therefore will I rather glory in my **infirmities**, that the power of Christ may rest upon me. Therefore I take pleasure in infirmities, in reproaches, in necessities, in persecutions, in distresses for Christ's sake: for when I am weak, then am I strong.* (2 Corinthians 12:7-10).

This is the only recorded prayer that Paul prays solely for himself!

FOUR things about Paul's prayer:

I. The DISCOMFORT stated in Paul's prayer.

Paul called his infirmity *"a thorn in the flesh."* We don't know exactly what this "thorn" was. We only know it was painful. It buffeted him.

- Have you ever been stuck with a thorn? [CHOLLA or CAT'S CLAW CACTUS!]
- As soon as we get stuck with a thorn, we want it removed as fast as possible. This is natural.

As painful as the thorn was, Paul did not whine about it. It led him to pray! As it says in James 5:13 — *"Is any among you afflicted? LET HIM PRAY!"*

II. The DETERMINATION of Paul's prayer.

Paul prayed **three times** for this thorn to be removed.

He *"besought"* (pleaded, begged) the Lord in prayer.

III. God's DENIAL to Paul's prayer.

What was God's answer to Paul's prayer? Essentially, it was, **"NO."**

- Instead of removing the thorn, God gave Paul grace to bear the thorn (v. 9 —

"And he said unto me, My grace is sufficient for thee: for my strength is made perfect in weakness.").

"No," is an answer. [6] (Also, "Not now.") Not all physical healing is the will of God (cf. 2 Timothy 4:21).

Sometimes saying "No" is the most loving answer you can give to a person's request. A "no" answer often shows you are looking out for a person's best interest.

IV. God's DESIGN of Paul's thorn.

Notice the thorn was *"given"* (v. 7), **not** SENT.

There is nothing wrong about wanting an infirmity removed. However, it becomes wrong when we **insist** it be removed, instead of recognizing that God has a purpose in giving the thorn to us.

There was **a reason** God allowed this thorn to be in Paul's flesh (v. 7). God has a purpose in our suffering.

---

[6] See Author's book, *David, A Man After God's Heart*, chapter 49.

Grace is the answer to all your problems (cf. 9:8). Grace will not SOLVE your problems, but it is the ANSWER to what you need for your problems. Grace does not *erase* your problems — It *eases* your problems. Grace does not *remove* your problems — It provides *relief* in your problems.

SUMMATION: God can take something unpleasant or painful and use it for His glory and our good.

PAUL'S PRAYERS #6 (Ephesians 1:15-23)

A Prayer of Three "Whats"

Wherefore I also, after I heard of your faith in the Lord Jesus, and love unto all the saints, Cease not to give thanks for you, making mention of you in my prayers; That the God of our Lord Jesus Christ, the Father of glory, may give unto you the spirit of wisdom and revelation in the knowledge of him: The eyes of your understanding being enlightened; that ye may know what is the hope of his calling, and what the riches of the glory of his inheritance in the saints, And what is the exceeding greatness of his power to us-ward who believe, according to the working of his mighty power, Which he wrought in Christ, when he raised him from the dead, and set him at his own right hand in the heavenly places, Far above all principality, and power, and might, and dominion, and every name that is named, not only in this world, but also in that which is to come: And hath put all things under his feet, and gave him to be the head over all things to the church, Which is his body, the fulness of him that filleth all in all. (Ephesians 1:15-23)

In 1949, Jack Wurm was broke and unemployed. One day, while he was walking along a San Francisco beach, he found a bottle with a note inside. As he read the note, he discovered it was the last will and testament of Daisy Singer Alexander, heir to the Singer sewing machine fortune. The note read: "To avoid confusion, I leave my entire estate to the lucky person who finds this bottle and to my attorney, Barry Cohen, share and share alike."

The courts accepted the theory the heiress wrote the note 12 years earlier, and tossed the bottle into the Thames River in London. It drifted across the oceans to a beach in San Francisco where Jack Wurm found it. His chance discovery netted him over 6 million dollars in cash and Singer stock. What a find!

And yet six million dollars doesn't begin to compare with our spiritual inheritance and riches in Christ!

God has laid up spiritual blessings for us in the Lord Jesus Christ (vs. 3, 11-14).

However, these blessings, will never profit a Christian during his earthly sojourn unless **he prays them in**.

➡ There are **two prayers** of Paul in Ephesians:

1) *"That ye might KNOW…"* (1:15-23). A **prayer for ENLIGHTENMENT.**

2) *"That he would grant you… to be strengthened…"* (3:14-21). **A prayer for ENPOWERMENT**. (Next chapter)

Paul's prayer in Ephesians 1:15-23 is a *lollapalooza*—jammed packed with spiritual blessings. It is the **longest** recorded prayer of Paul (one long sentence). It is A SEVEN-FOLD PRAYER:

1. Giving thanks (v. 16) — *"Cease not to give thanks for you, making mention of you in my prayers"*
2. That God would give them *"the spirit of wisdom and revelation…"*
3. That they would have *"…the knowledge of him"* — Spiritual things can only be discerned by spiritual means (1 Cor. 3:11-14).

4. That they would be enlightened (v. 18) – *"The eyes of your understanding being enlightened..."*
5. That they may know the hope of His calling (v. 18 – *"...that ye may know what is the hope of his calling..."*)
6. That they may know the riches of the glory of his inheritance (v. 18 – *"...what the riches of the glory of his inheritance in the saints"*).
7. That they may know the exceeding greatness of God's power to believers (vs. 19-20 – *"what is the exceeding greatness of his power to us-ward who believe, according to the working of his mighty power, which he wrought in Christ..."*).

Paul prays for somethings every Christian should KNOW (vs. 17, 18).

Know WHAT?

This is a prayer of **THREE "WHATS"** (vs. 18, 19).

I. The Knowledge of our PROSPECT.
"WHAT is the hope of his calling..." (v. 18).

We need to know the hope we have in Christ.

A. It is a HOPEFUL calling (1:18 cf. 4:4).

B. It is a HIGH calling (Phil. 3:14). *"I press toward the mark for the prize of THE HIGH CALLING of God in Christ Jesus."*

C. It is a HOLY calling (2 Tim. 1:9). *"Who hath saved us, and CALLED us with an HOLY CALLING..."*

D. It is a HEAVENLY calling (Heb. 3:1). *"Wherefore, holy brethren, partakers of the HEAVENLY CALLING..."*

II. The Knowledge of our PRECIOUSNESS (v. 18).

*"**WHAT** is the riches of the glory of his inheritance..."*

We need to know how valuable we are to God. God sees us as part of His great wealth. We are HIS inheritance!

"His INHERITANCE...
The GLORY of His INHERITANCE...
The RICHES of the GLORY of His INHERITANCE...
The RICHES of the GLORY of His INHERITANCE in the SAINTS."

III. The Knowledge of His POWER (vs. 19-23).

*"**WHAT** is the exceeding greatness of his power to us-ward..."*

We need to know the power we have in Christ.

This power is described in verses 20-23.

A. The **APPEARENCE** of His power: Resurrection power (v. 20 cf. 2:1, 5 cf. Romans 8:10-11).

B. The **AWESOMENESS** of His power (vs. 20-23; cf. Philippians 2:9-11).

"His POWER…
The GREATNESS of His power…
The EXCEEDING greatness of His power…
*The exceeding greatness of his power to **US-WARD**."*

1. We are seated at God the Father's right hand. *FAR above all…* (Geographically and authoritatively).

   - All **principality** and **power** and **might** and **dominion**. Satan, devils, angels, are all subject to Him (1 Peter 3:22).

   - Every name that is named: Satan, Trump, Biden, Putin.

   - In every age: Nimrod, Alexander the Great, Caesar, Hitler.

2. All are UNDER HIS FEET! (Geographically). The earth is His FOOTSTOOL!

C. The **ALTITUDE** of His power— *"to US-WARD… TO the church"* (vs. 19, 22).

WHAT A PRAYER!

SUMMATION: Years ago, a woman who lived in a remote valley in Wales, went to a great deal of trouble to have electrical power installed to her home. The electric company noticed she hardly used any electricity. Her usage was minuscule.

A meter reader was sent out to check it out. The meter man went to the door and said, "We've looked at the usage amount. Don't you use electricity?" "Oh yes" she said. "We turn it on every night to see how to light our lamps and then we switch it off again."

This sounds like the way many Christians apply the power of God in their lives!

Paul's Prayers #7 (Ephesians 3:14-21)

A Prayer for Inner Strength

For this cause I bow my knees unto the Father of our Lord Jesus Christ, Of whom the whole family in heaven and earth is named, That he would grant you, according to the riches of his glory, to be strengthened with might by his Spirit in the inner man; That Christ may dwell in your hearts by faith; that ye, being rooted and grounded in love, May be able to comprehend with all saints what is the breadth, and length, and depth, and height; And to know the love of Christ, which passeth knowledge, that ye might be filled with all the fulness of God. Now unto him that is able to do exceeding abundantly above all that we ask or think, according to the power that worketh in us, Unto him be glory in the church by Christ Jesus throughout all ages, world without end. Amen. (Ephesians 3:14-21)

As mentioned in the previous chapter, there are two prayers of Paul in Ephesians:

1) *"That ye might KNOW..."* (1:15-23). **A prayer for ENLIGHTENMENT.**

2) *"That he would grant you… to be strengthened"* (3:14-21). **A prayer for ENPOWERMENT**.

In Ephesians 1:17, Paul addresses his prayer to *"the GOD of our Lord Jesus Christ."* But, in Ephesians 3:14 Paul bows his knees in prayer to *"the FATHER of our Lord Jesus Christ."* We approach God in prayer by the merits of the Lord Jesus Christ.

Paul's prayer in Ephesians 1 was a **prayer of three "whats."** His prayer in Ephesians 3 is a **prayer of three "thats."**

- v. 16— *"THAT he would grant you…"*
- v. 17— *"THAT Christ may dwell in your hearts by faith…"* Obviously, Christ was already in their hearts (Galatians 2:20). *"Dwell"* means "to be at home." Does He have absolute liberty to go wherever He pleases?
- v. 17— *"THAT ye, being rooted and grounded in love, may be able to…"*

Paul is kneeling on the floor of his prison (v. 14, *"bow my knees"* —posture of humility).

Paul prays for *the inner man* to be *"strengthened"* (v. 16; Philippians 1:9-11; Colossians 1:9-11). God's emphasis is upon *"the inner man"* (cf. 2 Corinthians 4:16). Most people focus on the outward man. If *"the inner man"* is right with God, the *"outward man"* will take care of itself!

I. REQUEST for strength (3:14-16, 20 cf. Philippians 4:13).

We need God's strength – *"strengthened with might* [GK. dunamis=dynamite] *BY HIS SPIRIT."*

A. It is impossible to live the Christian life in your own strength (6:10).

B. Example of Jesus (Luke 4:1, 14; Acts 10:38). Jesus said, *"I can of mine own self do nothing..."* (John 5:30).

C. Pray for your brothers and sisters in Christ to be strengthened.

II. RATIO of strength (3:16)

Not "out of his riches," but *"according to his riches."*

A. God always supplies *"according to"* (see Ephesians 1:19; 3:20; Philippians 4:19; Colossians 1:11, 29).

B. If I'm a millionaire and give you $10, I have given you *out* of my riches. If I give you $10,000, I have given you *"according to my riches."*

III. ROOTS of strength (3:17)

We are strengthened by *"being rooted and grounded in love."*

A. Roots provide nourishment and stability to a tree. Knowing the love of God will nourish and **stabilize** the saint.

B. The DIMENSIONS of God's love:[7]

1. God's love is WIDE (*"breadth"*). It reaches everyone in the whole world.

2. God's love is LONG (*"length"*). When did God start loving us? When will He stop loving us? It is an everlasting, infinite love.

3. God's love is DEEP (*"depth"*). It goes to the depths of our discouragements, despair, and even death.

4. God's love is HIGH (*"height"*). It rises above every circumstance (cf. Romans 8:38-39).

---

[7] See Author's book, *God is Love*, "The Geometry of God's Love."

C. Knowing *"the love of Christ which passes knowledge"* (v. 19).

1. There is **knowable** love of Christ.

    a. The faithfulness of His love. He always loves us.

    b. The forgiveness of His love. He always forgives us.

    c. The fellowship of His love. Nothing separates us from His love.

2. There is the love of Christ that is **unknowable**: We can know the expression, but we will never know it's essence. God is love.

SUMMATION (Benediction vs. 20-21): **Enablement**

God... (Starts with God).

*God **is able**...* (God is capable).

*God is able to **do**...* (He is not only capable, he will take action to perform).

*God is able to do **exceeding**...* (to surpass).

*God is able to do exceeding **abundantly**...* (to overflow).

*God is able to do exceeding abundantly **above**...* (to go over and above).

*God is able to do exceeding abundantly above **all we ask**... (No matter what we ask for).

God is able to do exceeding abundantly above all we ask or THINK,* (Our brain is not capable of imagining something God cannot do!)

Too often we sell the Lord short by praying for too little. To be sure, God is interested in EVERY request (great or small). But BIG prayers honor God's ability more than small prayers.

God said in Psalm 81:10, *"I am the LORD thy God, which brought thee out of the land of Egypt: **open thy mouth wide, and I will fill it.**"* Jeremiah 33:3, *"Call unto me, and I will answer thee, and shew thee **great and mighty things,** which thou knowest not."* [8]

Bottom line — Amen! (v. 21). Let's pray for our brothers and sisters in Christ to be strengthened... to be rooted in the love of Christ... and to know how powerful God is!

---

[8] John R. Rice, *Prayer: Asking and Receiving (Classic Edition)*, Sword of the Lord Publishers, Murfreesboro, TN. 1970, pp. 195-212.

Paul's Prayers #8 (Philippians 1:9-11)

A Prayer for Love to be Regulated by Knowledge

And this I pray, that your love may abound yet more and more in knowledge and in all judgment; That ye may approve things that are excellent; that ye may be sincere and without offence till the day of Christ; Being filled with the fruits of righteousness, which are by Jesus Christ, unto the glory and praise of God. (Philippians 1:9-11)

Philippians is a prison epistle of Paul. Paul wrote **five epistles while in prison (prison epistles)**:
1. Ephesians 3:1; 4:1
2. Philippians 1:7, 13-16
3. Colossians 4:10, 18
4. Philemon 1:1, 9
5. 2 Timothy 1:8, 16

While in prison Paul prays for the saints at Philippi— *"And this I pray…"*

- Prison may cut a man off from his friends, but it cannot cut him off from God!

- Paul prays **specifically**… (*"THAT…"*)
A Four-fold prayer:

I. Paul prays the Philippians would have an ABOUNDING love (v. 9).

Abounding love is **not static** — It **grows** *"more and more."* (1 Thessalonians 3:12 – *"And the Lord make you **to INCREASE and ABOUND in love one toward another…"***).

Abounding Biblical love is **discerning** (*"…in knowledge and in all judgment"*). Biblical love is **not the senseless** emotional slop as portrayed in Hollywood (1 Corinthians 13).

Biblical love teaches us what to love and what not to love — To love what God loves and hate what God hates. The more we love the Lord, the more we will choose the things that are excellent and best for Him.

The more we love each other, the more we will choose the excellent and best for each other. An abounding love will not want to do anything that would cause someone to stumble.

II. Paul prays the Philippians would APPROVE things that are excellent (v. 10 cf. Romans 2:18).

- Some things are *"excellent"* and other things are not. Paul prays for their ability to discern between right and wrong… good and bad… healthy and hazardous… good and the best… and important and urgent.
- How do you tell the difference? By approving them.

> *"Approve"* (root word "prove"). It means "to put it to the test." (cf. Ephesians 5:10 — *"PROVING what is acceptable unto the Lord"*; 1 Thessalonians 5:21 — *"PROVE all things; hold fast that which is good"*).

- Things that *excel* are found in Philippians 4 and 1 Corinthians 13 (see 1 Corinthians 12:31).

III. Paul prays the Philippians would be AUTHENTIC and without offense (v. 10).

"What you see is what you get." Transparent — **Unfeigned** - 1 Peter 1:22

- *That ye may be **sincere** and without offence.* The word *sincere* is from the Latin word "sinceritas," and is a metaphor of something that is pure, like pure honey. When held up to the light, it is found without any wax or honeycomb in it.
- When we hold our lives up to the light of God's Word, there should not be anything that would distort our relationship with God, or dim our witness for of Christ.
- Being sincere without being offensive. Not easy to do.

IV. Paul prays the Philippians would be ABUNDANT in fruitfulness (v. 11).

Different varieties of fruit:

1) Fruits of **righteousness** (v. 10; Proverbs 11:30; Romans 1:13).
2) Fruits of **labor** (v. 22; Colossians 1:10).
3) Fruit of the **Gospel** (Colossians 1:5-6).
4) Fruit of the **Spirit** (Galatians 5:22-23).
5) Fruits of **repentance** (Matthew 3:8).
6) Fruits of **identification** (Matthews 7:17-20).
7) Fruits of **resurrection** (1 Corinthians 15:20-24).

SUMMATION: Let us pray for each other that…

(1) our love may ABOUND, and

(2) APPROVE what is excellent, and

(3) that we might be AUTHENTIC, and

(4) ABUNDANT in fruitfulness.

Paul's Prayers #9 (Colossians 1:9-12)

Prayer for a Worthy Walk

For this cause we also, since the day we heard it, do not cease to pray for you, and to desire that ye might be filled with the knowledge of his will in all wisdom and spiritual understanding; That ye might walk worthy of the Lord unto all pleasing, being fruitful in every good work, and increasing in the knowledge of God; strengthened with all might, according to his glorious power, unto all patience and longsuffering with joyfulness; Giving thanks unto the Father, which hath made us meet to be partakers of the inheritance of the saints in light: (Colossians 1:9-12).

As far as we know, Paul never visited Colosse. Epaphras told Paul about the church at Colosse: About their faith (v. 4); their love for one another (v. 4); and their love in the Spirit (v. 8).

➡ *"For this cause WE also, since the day WE heard it, do not cease to pray for you…"* This was a prayer that was prayed **jointly** by Paul and his companions (Timothy-

Philippians 1:1; Ehaphras-Colossians 1:7; Philemon 23).

This prayer **hinges** on the word *"THAT"* in verse 10. A **full** [9] knowledge and understanding of God's will (v. 9) is **essential** to *"walk worthy of the Lord…"*

- For example: How can I "walk worthy of the Lord" if I am not "filled with the knowledge of His will"? It is impossible!
- Too many Christians are either ignorant or they don't care about God's will. They are mainly concerned about their own will.

  > ***"That ye might WALK WORTHY of the Lord…"*** This objective is very challenging for me to wrap my puny mind around!

- Paul exhorted the Ephesians, *"That ye walk **worthy** of the vocation wherewith ye are called…"* (Ephesians 4:1).
- 1 Thessalonians 2:12, *"That ye would walk **worthy** of God…"*

---

[9] That they might not merely know God's will, but that they might be FILLED with it!

- 2 Thessalonians 1:5, *"…that ye may be counted **worthy** of the kingdom of God, for which ye also suffer…"*
- In Acts 5:40-41, after the apostles were beaten and commanded not to *"speak in the name of Jesus… they departed from the presence of the council, rejoicing **that they were counted WORTHY to suffer for His name."***

> *"**THAT ye might WALK WORTHY of the Lord…**"* Your *"walk"* is how you live or conduct yourself. ***"Walk"*** indicates your behavior.

Who can HONESTLY say they WALK WORTHY OF CHRIST — of His teachings… His example… His Cross? Jacob said, ***"I am NOT WORTHY of the least of all thy mercies…"*** (Genesis 32:10). Revelation 5:2-4, *"Who is **WORTHY** to open the book? … And no man in heaven, nor in earth, neither under the earth, was able to open the book… And I wept much, because no man was found **WORTHY** to open and to read the book."*

According to the *Webster 1828 Dictionary,* ***"worthy"*** means… Deserving or possessing qualities suited to.

No one is *deserving* of Christ or possess qualities suited to Christ. **But,** we may act suitably to our relationship with the Christ, whose name we bear (Ephesians 5:3; Philippians 1:27 — ***"Let your conversation be as it becometh the gospel of Christ...")***

Notice what Paul prays...

1. We walk worthy of the Lord by **pleasing the Lord** (v. 10 cf. Hebrews 11:6). Everything we do either pleases God or displeases God. Our actions either honor the Lord or dishonor the Lord.
2. We walk worthy of the Lord by *"being fruitful in every good work..."* (v. 10 cf. John 15:8 — *"Herein is my Father glorified, that ye bear much fruit..."*
3. We walk worthy of the Lord by ***"increasing in the knowledge of God"*** (v. 10).
4. We walk worthy of the Lord by being *"***strengthen****ed with all might according to his glorious power..."* (v. 11a). I cannot walk worthily of the Lord in my own strength. I desperately need His power.
5. We walk worthy of the Lord by being **patient and longsuffering with joyfulness** (v. 11b). *"Longsuffering with*

joyfulness" is the capacity to endure a stressful situation over a long period of time without complaining about it.

SUMMATION: We should pattern our prayers after Paul's prayers.

How to Pray for Other Christians:

1) Thank God for them (1:3).
2) Pray for them to be filled with the knowledge of God's will (1:9a).
3) Pray for their spiritual understanding (1:9b).
4) Pray that they would walk worthy of the Lord (1:10a).
5) Pray that they would be fruitful (1:10b).
6) Pray for them to grow in their knowledge of God (1:10c).
7) Pray for God to strengthen them (1:11a).
8) Pray for them to be patient and joyful (1:11b).
9) Pray for them to be thankful (1:12).

How many of your prayers measure up to this pattern?

Paul's Prayers #10 (1 Thessalonians 3:9-13)

A Prayer for New Converts

For what thanks can we render to God again for you, for all the joy wherewith we joy for your sakes before our God; Night and day praying exceedingly that we might see your face, and might perfect that which is lacking in your faith? Now God himself and our Father, and our Lord Jesus Christ, direct our way unto you. And the Lord make you to increase and abound in love one toward another, and toward all men, even as we do toward you To the end he may stablish your hearts unblameable in holiness before God, even our Father, at the coming of our Lord Jesus Christ with all his saints. (1 Thessalonians 3:9-13)

1. The **CONTEXT**: Chronologically, this is the first recorded prayer of Paul in Scripture.

Paul founded the church at Thessalonica in **Acts 17**. He was *"sent away"* (probably run out of town) from Thessalonica (Acts 17:10).

He wrote this epistle from Athens [10] (Acts 17:16 - 18:1).

2. The **CIRCUMSTANCE**:

Paul was compelled to leave Thessalonica before he could establish these young converts in the Word (Acts 17:10 cf. 1 Thessalonians 2:17).

The "follow-up" of new converts is important — 1 and 2 Thessalonians are letters to new converts. [11]

It was so important that Paul sent Timotheus to continue to establish these new believers (3:1-2).

➡ Note the repeated reference to *"your faith"* in 3:2, 5, 7, 10 cf. 2 Thessalonians 1:3). The faith of these new believers was a great concern to Paul. Something was still lacking in their faith (3:10).

3. The **CONCERN**:

The **intensity** of Paul's prayer for these new believers. Verse 10 — *"Night and day praying exceedingly..."* (2:9). How we also

---

[10] See the post-script at the end of 1 Thessalonians.
[11] These two letters deal with all the basics of the Christian life.

need to have this same intense interest in new converts.

The Thessalonians were under severe persecution (1:6: 2:14). The Thessalonians remained faithful to the Lord in spite of persecution. This good news was a comfort to Paul (3:6-9 cf. 3 John 3-4 — *"For I rejoiced greatly, when the brethren came and testified of the truth that is in thee, even as thou walkest in truth. **I have no greater joy than to hear that my children walk in truth.**"*).

Too often we are more interested in hearing bad news than good news. Not Paul (v. 9). We should be more eager to hear about Christians growing, not backsliding.

4. The **CONTENT: Three petitions** of Paul's prayer...

First, Paul prayed the Lord would direct his way back to Thessalonica to *"perfect that which is lacking in* [their] *faith"* (vs. 10-12).

- Direction (guidance) from the Lord (Jeremiah 10:23; Proverbs 3:5-6).
- Satan hindered Paul's return (2:18).

Second, Paul prayed for their love to grow and abound (v. 12). Not only a love for one another, but also for ALL MEN (v. 12).

- Only the Lord can produce this kind of love— *"And the Lord MAKE you to increase and abound in love…"* God answered this prayer (2 Thessalonians 1:3).
- May our prayer be the same as Paul's—*"Lord make [us] to increase and abound in love one toward another…"* Our actions should display our love. *"Let us not love in word, neither in tongue, but in DEED and in truth"* (1 John 3:18).
- When the Jews saw Jesus weep at the tomb of Lazarus, they said, ***"Behold how he loved him!*** (John 11:36). May this be said of us, "Behold how they love one another!"

Thirdly, verse 13— ***"To the end…"*** (purpose). Paul prayed that their hearts would be established unblameable in holiness at the coming of the Lord Jesus Christ (v. 13).

Paul's Prayers #11 (1 Thessalonians 5:23)

A Prayer for Sanctification and Preservation

And the very God of peace sanctify you wholly; and I pray God your whole spirit and soul and body be preserved blameless unto the coming of our Lord Jesus Christ. (1 Thessalonians 5:23)

The general idea of sanctification is separateness. There is **positional** sanctification that occurs the moment a person trusts Christ for salvation (This is our **standing before God** – 1 Corinthians 1:30). There is also **practical** sanctification (on-going) as a Christian yields himself to Christ. This is our **standing before men**.

The same is true regarding our PRESERVATION in Christ. He preserves (protects; keeps) us (Psalm 140:1-4; 2 Timothy 4:18). Jude 1:24 says, *"Now unto him that is able to KEEP you from falling, and to present you FAULTLESS before the presence of his glory and exceeding joy."* [12]

Paul prays the Thessalonians will live outwardly what God is doing inwardly.

The **TRINITY OF MAN** (TRICHOTOMY)

Man is created in the image of God as a triune being—He is **spirit, soul, and body**. (See Larkin chart - **APPENDIX 1**).

1. First—**Spirit** (God conscious). Corresponds to the **HEART.**
2. Second–**Soul** (Self-conscious—The seat of emotions, will, and intellect). Corresponds to the **HEAD** (mind).
3. Third–**Body** (The outward man that is world conscious). Corresponds to the **HAND.**

➡**Sanctification** involves all of these:

- **Spirit** – Keep your focus on Jesus.
- **Soul** – Keep your mind off of yourself.

---

[12] The New Testament saint can do nothing to preserve himself or keep himself saved. However, he can do something about being *"blameless."* Blameless does not mean sinless perfection. It means living above reproach so the unsaved crowd can have nothing to say against our testimony for Christ.

- **Body**—Keep your body away from the world.

Notice the **Scriptural order**: Spirit—Soul—Body. This is the Divine order of priorities for a Christian.

Sometimes we reverse the order by saying: "Body, soul, and spirit." God's order is spirit, **first**; soul, **second**; and body **last**. God starts with the **inner** most part of our being and **works outward** (like the plan to build the tabernacle – Exodus 25:9-10).

Consider the following various sequences of order:

SPIRIT / SOUL / BODY

- These are priorities of a sanctified Christian walking in the Spirit.
- He puts spiritual things first (Galatians 5:16).
- Denies the flesh.
- Has the fruit of the Spirit.

SPIRIT / BODY / SOUL

- These are priorities of a nominal Christian.
- He prioritizes the spirit, but he tends to satisfy the flesh.

- Doesn't like to study (soul last).
- The subject of the parable in Luke 8:14.

BODY / SPIRIT / SOUL

- The priorities of a carnal Christian (maybe unsaved).
- Puts the body before the spiritual. He is governed by the flesh.
- Worldly / Sensual. Well groomed (cosmetics; clothes).
- He likes a religion that appeals to his emotions and flesh.
- He usually lacks discipline in finances; schedule; and religious responsibility.
- Described in 1 Corinthians 3:1-3.

SOUL / SPIRIT / BODY

- Possibly a Christian (spiritual things second). He prioritizes his mind.
- He is probably a liberal / intellectual — Maybe a doctor, lawyer, teacher.
- Perhaps a follower of a "new age" cult.
- Described in Proverbs 14:12.

SOUL / BODY / SPIRIT

- Probably unsaved. Little interest in the things of the Spirit.

- Head and hand emphasized — Heart is neglected.
- Prefers a social-gospel type religion.
- Described in 2 Timothy 3:2-7.

BODY / SOUL / SPIRIT

- Unsaved. He puts his body and soul (mind) ahead of anything spiritual. Jude 1:19 says, *"These be they who separate themselves, SENSUAL, having not the SPIRIT."*
- Spiritually dead (Ephesians 2:1).
- No interest in spiritual things like church, prayer, faith, or the Bible (cf. 1 Corinthians 2:14 — *"The natural man receiveth NOT the things of the Spirit of God: for they are foolishness unto him: neither can he know them, because they are spiritually discerned."*)
- Hedonistic. Lover of pleasure more than lover of God.
- A humanist. Maybe a liberal politician or business man. Peter and Jude liken this man to *"natural brute beasts"* (2 Peter. 2:10-12; Jude 1:10).
- Described in Romans 1:21-32.

ILLUSTRATION: A burning candle has three parts: (1) A body of wax; (2) the wick; (3) the flame. The wax represents our body; the wick is our mind; the flame is the spirit. As long as the flame is higher than the body, it burns brightly, but if the candle is turned over, the light will flicker and go out.

We must keep the order right: SPIRIT on top; SOUL second; BODY last.

Paul's Prayers #12 (2 Thessalonians 1:11-12)

A Prayer for a Persecuted Church

Wherefore also we pray always for you, that God would count you worthy of this calling, and fulfil all the good pleasure of his goodness, and the work of faith with power: That the name of our Lord Jesus Christ may be glorified in you, and ye in him, according to the grace of our God and the Lord Jesus Christ. (2 Thessalonians 1:11-12)

As we learned in a previous chapter, Paul is writing to a young church that was going through the furnace of affliction (1 Thessalonians 1:6: 2:14). Their faithfulness to God while enduring persecution provides a **context** for Paul's prayer.

"Wherefore also..." Paul's prayer (vs. 11-12) is based on what he previously wrote in verses 3-10 (one long sentence, read these):

1. He thanks God for their growing faith (1:3 cf. 1 Thessalonians 3:2, 5, 6, 7, 10).

2 He thanks God for their abounding *"charity"* (1:3 cf. 1 Thessalonians 3:12).

3. He boasted to other churches about their patience and faith during persecution (1:4).

4. Their persecution was evidence God counted them worthy (cf. Acts 5:40-42; Philippians 1:28-29).

   - The enemies of Christians often misinterpret troubles as evidence of God's judgment against Christians, or that they are not really saved. However, Christians should view tribulations as confirmation they are truly saved (cf. Philippians 1;28-30; Hebrews 12:5-11; 1 Peter 4:12-19).

5. God will recompense tribulation to whoever troubled them (vs. 6-8).

   - For example: God used Assyria and Babylon as instruments to chasten Israel. Then He turned the table and judged Assyria and Babylon for the affliction they brought against Israel (Isaiah 10:12, 24-26; Jeremiah 25:3-12).
   - Bob Jones, Sr. said, "A holy God will even everything out." Amen! As

Abraham said, *"**Shall not the Judge of all the earth do right?**"* (Genesis 18:23) The wicked will not get away with troubling God's people.

6. The church at Thessalonica should relax (*"rest with us"*) knowing Jesus will avenge them at His return (vs. 6-9).

Because of these things (*"**Wherefore…**"*), Paul prays (vs. 11-12):

First, Paul does NOT pray for them to be delivered from persecution. Paul prays knowing that the persecuted church at Thessalonica is counted *"worthy of this calling"* (cf. v. 5). The *"calling"* Paul refers to is a call to suffer now and be glorified when Christ returns (v. 10).

Second, Paul prays for the fulfillment of *"all **the good pleasure of his goodness,** and the work of faith with power"* (v. 11).

- God will complete what He began in the Thessalonians (Philippians 1:6- *"Being confident of this very thing, that **he which hath BEGUN a good work in you will perform it** until the day of Jesus Christ."* cf. 1 Corinthians 1:8). God ain't through with me yet! Praise the Lord!

God is still working *"his good pleasure"* in me. Philippians 2:13, *"For it is God which worketh in you both to will and to do of **his good pleasure**."*

Third, *"that the name of our Lord Jesus **Christ may be glorified in you**, and ye in him…"* The bottom line is, everything we do is for the glory of God (1 Corinthians 10:31; Colossians 3:17).

- Ultimately, the Lord will be glorified by His saints as they are displayed as trophies of His grace when He returns. Ephesians 2:7, *"That in the ages to come he might **show the exceeding riches of his grace in his kindness toward us** through Christ Jesus."* Christ will *"be **admired**"* at His coming by the faithfulness of the Thessalonians (v. 10).
- What is there in your life that Christ will be admired for?

Paul's Prayers #13 (2 Timothy 1:16; 4:14-15)

A Prayer for an ALLY and an ADVERSARY

The Lord give mercy unto the house of **Onesiphorus**; *for he oft refreshed me, and was not ashamed of my chain: But, when he was in Rome, he sought me out very diligently, and found me. The Lord grant unto him that he may find mercy of the Lord in that day: and in how many things he ministered unto me at Ephesus, thou knowest very well. (2 Timothy 1:16-18)*

Alexander *the coppersmith did me much evil: the Lord reward him according to his works: Of whom be thou ware also; for he hath greatly withstood our words. (2 Timothy 4:14-15)*

2 Timothy is the last inspired epistle Paul wrote. It is one of the "pastoral epistles" (1 & 2 Timothy and Titus).

According to the *post-script* at the end of 2 Timothy,[13] Timothy was now the pastor of

---

[13] *"The second epistle unto Timotheus, ordained the first bishop of the church of the Ephesians, was written from Rome, when Paul was brought before Nero the second time."*

the church at Ephesus. Paul wrote this epistle while imprisoned in Rome, shortly before the Emperor Nero had Paul beheaded.

Paul prays for a **friend** (Onesiphorus) in 1:16-18 and a **foe** (Alexander, the coppersmith) in 4:14-15. What a contrast in these two men. Everything Onesiphorous was to Paul, Alexander was NOT. Onesiphorus REFRESHED Paul — Alexander RESISTED Paul.

Let's see what we can learn from these two prayers of Paul.

I. **Prayer for an ALLY** (2 Timothy 1:16-18).

➡ When many turned away from Paul (1:15 cf. 4:10-16), Paul had a close friend in Onesiphorus.[14]

➡ A friend is one who comes in when the whole world has gone out.

---

[14] Sometimes we tend to think we have been abandoned and left alone (1 Kings 19:10, 14, 18). This is how Paul felt, but he was not alone (2 Timothy 4:16, 21).

1) Paul prays for his **FAMILY** (v. 16 - *"...the house of..."* cf. 4:19).[15]
2) Paul prays about his **FORTITUDE** (v. 16- *"...was not ashamed of my chain..."*)
3) Paul prays about his **FRIENDSHIP** (v. 17 - *"...when he was in Rome, he sought me out very diligently, and found me"*). He came from Ephesus to visit Paul in prison.
   ➥ What a great friend! I hope you have a friend like Onesiphorus. Or, you can be a friend like Onesiphorus.
4) Paul prays about his **FAITHFULNESS** (v. 16 - ***oft*** *refreshed me...* v. 18 - *how **many times** he ministered unto me..."*). Onesiphorus was a faithful servant (Matthew 25:21). This is someone that everyone can be!
   ➥ "Onesiphorus" literally means "a bringer of profit." Ask yourself, "Who am I profitable to?"

---

[15] Herbert Lockyer, on page 259 of his book *All the Prayers of the Bible*, says Onesiphorus was probably dead when Paul wrote 2 Timothy. Lockyer says this because Paul was actually praying for the *house* of Onesiphorus. [I personally believe that Onesiphorus was still alive.]

5) Paul prays about his **FAME** (v. 18- *"thou knowest very well."*). He had a good testimony before others.

Because of these things, Paul asked the Lord to extend mercy to Onesiphorus at the Judgment Seat of Christ (v. 18).

II. Prayer for an ADVERSARY (2 Timothy 4:14-15).

1) Paul had many enemies. One of Paul's adversaries was *"Alexander the coppersmith."* Since Timothy was a pastor in Ephesus, this was probably the same Alexander in Acts 19:33-34 and 1 Timothy 1:19-20. [16]
2) Paul often **named** those who turned away from him (cf. 1 Timothy 1:19-20; 2 Timothy 1:15; 4:10; Titus 1:10-13). This was John's practice also (3 John 9-10).
3) Alexander did Paul much evil. He withstood Paul's preaching.
4) Jesus said to **pray for your enemies** (Matthew 5:44).

---

[16] 1 Timothy 1:20 - Alexander was a common name during the first century.

- Paul's prayer — *"the Lord reward him according to his works."* Paul prays for God to give Alexander what he had coming to him (see 2 Samuel 3:39; Psalm 28:4).
- Paul prays for God's mercy for Onesiphorus' family, and prays for God to render justice to Alexander.
- Paul turned Alexander over to the devil to deal with him (1 Timothy 1:20). This is a good policy when praying for an enemy.

5) Paul also **warned** Timothy about Alexander (v. 15). He cautioned Timothy to beware him — He's a trouble-maker. Philippians 3:2, *"Beware of dogs, **beware of evil workers**, beware of the concision."*

Paul's Prayers #14 (2 Timothy 4:16)

Praying for Deserters

At my first answer no man stood with me, but all men forsook me: **I pray God that it may not be laid to their charge.** *Notwithstanding the Lord stood with me, and strengthened me; that by me the preaching might be fully known, and that all the Gentiles might hear: and I was delivered out of the mouth of the lion. (2 Timothy 4:16-17)*

Many believers bailed-out on Paul when the heat was on. He felt all alone, but then realized the Lord was still with him. Praise God.

Deserting fellow believers when they are being persecuted is a common occurrence among thin skinned Christians. They cannot stand the heat, so they "jump-ship." Many of Jesus' disciples did the same thing (John 6:60-71; Matthew 26:56).

While I was serving as a pastor in a couple of local churches, I remember times when some of my so-called friends turned their backs on me in the heat of a battle.

How should we pray for these who abandon us when the going gets rough? Note how Paul prays, ***"I pray God that it may not be laid to their charge."*** Paul must have had a lot of grace to pray like this (Ephesians 4:32; Colossians 3:13; 1 Peter 3:9).

> Joseph Parker, a powerful preacher and contemporary of Charles Spurgeon, spent a great deal of time, especially in his younger years, speaking in public parks and gathering places, presenting the gospel to atheists and skeptics who gathered to discuss the topics of the day. Once he was confronted by an infidel who shouted at him, "What did God do for Stephen when he was stoned?" Parker responded, "He gave him grace to pray for those who stoned him."

- Paul's prayer is patterned after the way Jesus prayed when Roman soldiers nailed

Him to the cross: *"Father, forgive them; for they know not what they do"* (Luke 23:34). Those Roman soldiers were only following orders.

- No doubt, the dying prayer of Stephen had a profound impact of Paul as he witnessed Stephen being stoned (Acts 7:58-60 — *"Lord, lay not this sin to their charge"*).

Paul's Prayers #15 (2 Corinthians 13:14)

Paul's Prayer of Benediction

The grace of the Lord Jesus Christ, and the love of God, and the communion of the Holy Ghost, be with you all. Amen. (2 Corinthians 13:14)

Paul closes his second epistle to the Corinthians as it began — with a beautiful **benediction** (cf. 1:2-4). A benediction is simply a prayer that pronounces a blessing.[17]

- Benedictions are also found in Numbers 6:23-26 and 1 Peter 5:10-11.

> Donald Barnhouse would sometimes dismiss a church service with this benediction: "Now go in the peace of God the Father, and God the Son, and God the Holy Spirit, if you are a believer. And if you are not a

---

[17] A.W. Pink writes, "A **doxology** is an ascription of praise, a **benediction** is a word of blessing; the one ascends from the heart of the saint to God, the other descends from God to the saint." Samuel Chadwick wrote, "Consequently the benediction does not approach the subject from the standpoint of theology but of experience." (A.W. Pink, *Gleanings from Paul.*)

> believer, may your heart remain restless, may you be miserable, unhappy, lonely, and empty, until your heart finds rest in Jesus. Amen." Some of Barnhouse's church members did not appreciate his blunt honesty!

Our text is commonly called the **"Trinitarian benediction**."[18] It clearly summarizes the doctrinal truth of the Trinity.[19] The Trinity is three **persons** existing as one **being**—**GOD** (see diagram).

Our text is a prayer for Christians to live according to grace of the Lord Jesus Christ,

---

[18] God never commanded this benediction to be pronounced at the close of religious services, although I see nothing wrong with it.
[19] The Trinity is alluded to at Christ's baptism (Matthew 3:16-17) and in the baptismal formula (Matthew 28:19).

and the love of God, and the communion of the Holy Ghost. Where would we be without *"the grace of the Lord Jesus Christ"* or *"the love of God"* or *"the communion of the Holy Ghost"*? We would be lost!

NOTICE THE ORDER:

1. GRACE is **RECEIVED**… then
2. The LOVE of God is **REALIZED** and
3. The COMMUNION of the Holy Ghost is **RECIPROCATED**.
    - ➡ It all starts with *"the grace of the Lord Jesus Christ."* **Grace** then leads to God's **love** and God's love leads to **communion**[20] (fellowship).

It is only by **grace** that we can experience God's love for us. As a person realizes God's **love** for them they enter into the sweet **communion** with the Holy Ghost.

> **Communion** is the root word to *communication*. The Holy Ghost is *communicated* to the believer as he receives the grace of the Lord Jesus

---

[20] The word ***"communion"*** only occurs three times in a King James Bible (1 Corinthians 10:16; 2 Corinthians 6:14; 13:14. Each time it is translated from the Greek word "koinonia" which means fellowship.

> Christ and responds to the love God displayed at Calvary.
>
> The Holy Ghost immediately joins the Christian to the body of Christ (1 Corinthians 12:12-13). This makes abiding fellowship possible for the Holy Spirit and all fellow Christians (John 14:16-17; Romans 8:14-17; Philippians 2:1).

- As a person trusts Christ for salvation, they may also experience the **communion** with the Holy Ghost. While every Christian is indwelt by the Holy Ghost [21] (Romans 8:9-11; 1 Corinthians 3:16), not every believer is in fellowship with the Holy Ghost. The Holy Ghost is a PERSON.

SPECIFICALLY...

1. *"The **GRACE** of the Lord Jesus Christ..."* – Christ denied His own needs to die for our sins on Calvary. That same grace gives the Christian the same **CAPACITY**

---

[21] It is impossible for a person who is unsaved to have fellowship with the Holy Ghost.

to deny self for the benefit of another (cf. 2 Corinthians 8:9).

2. *"...and the **LOVE** of God..."* – It was the love God that sent His Son to provide a way for undeserving to be saved (Romans 5:8- *"But God commendeth his love toward us, in that, while we were yet sinners, Christ died for us."*). We must have that same **COMPASSION** towards the underserving. We love others with an unconditional love.

3. *"...and the **COMMUNION** of the Holy Ghost..."* **COMMUNION** is fellowship and involves a relationship (Philippians 2:1). That relationship should be nurtured and cultivated. As a Divine Person, the Holy Ghost may be lied to (Acts 5:3)! He can be grieved (Ephesians 4:30). He calls servants into His harvest (Acts 13:2-4). He can be talked to (Matthew 9:38; 1 Corinthians 14:14; Jude 1:20)! He can guide us where we should go, or not go (Acts 8:29; 16:6-10). He can be loved (Romans 15:30)!

A person may have a relationship with a parent, but, at the same time, be out of fellowship with a parent. Likewise, not

every believer enjoys the sweet
communion of the Spirit of God.

Dr. Walter Wilson (1881-1969), was a
medical doctor who became a Christian,
author, and pastored the Calvary Bible
Church in Kansas City. But, for a time,
his ministry bore little fruit. He was
once confronted by a missionary to
France who asked Dr. Wilson, "What is
the Holy Spirit to you?" Wilson
promptly answered, "The Holy Spirit is
the third person of the triune Godhead."
The missionary then said, "What you
said is true, but you did not answer my
question. I asked, 'What is the Holy
Spirit TO YOU?' Dr. Wilson was
speechless as he considered the
question. Finally, he admitted, "He is
nothing TO ME." Then the missionary
said, "That is why your ministry is
bearing little fruit." From that point on,
the ministry of Dr. Walter Wilson was
transformed. He began to fellowship
with the Spirit and walk *"in the Spirit."*
He went on to write several books
recounting his soul winning experiences
(*Strange Short Stories by the Doctor, Let's
Go Fishing, Just What the Doctor Ordered,*

Romance of a Doctor's Visits, Miracles in a Doctor's Life, etc.)

It is one thing to be *indwelt* by the Holy Spirit (John 20:22). It is another thing to be "*filled* with the Spirit" (Acts 2:4; 4:8, 31; Ephesians 5:18).

Paul's prayer of benediction is for every believer to live according to…

1. The **grace** of the Lord Jesus Christ.
2. The **unconditional love** of God.
3. The **communion** of the Holy Ghost.

EPILOG: Paul's Prayer Requests

1 Thessalonians 5:25 – *Brethren, pray for us.*

2 Corinthians 1:11 – *"Ye also HELPING together by prayer for us…"*

Since the Paul requested people to pray for him, how much more do we need people praying for us? He was an Apostle, yet he requested people to pray for him. When we pray for others, we are HELPING them in their ministry. What a blessing to know that people are remembering me in their prayers.

There are several specific prayer requests Paul asked for…

1. Romans 10:1 – *Brethren, my heart's desire and prayer to God for Israel is, that they might be saved.*

The SUBJECT. Paul prays for Israel to be saved. He knew that, in spite of their many privileges, they were lost because they rejected Christ.

- Salvation is our greatest need. No greater intercessory prayer could be offered than for the salvation of lost loved ones.

The SINCERITY (*"my heart's desire"*). What a burden Paul had for his *"kinsmen according to the flesh"* (9:1). Paul's passion for lost souls is evident (see Acts 20:19; 1 Thessalonians 2:16). Too often our praying is not sincere. Too often our prayer is for show and is hypocritical.

- What is your *"heart's desire?"* What consumes your thoughts?

One day, Paul's prayer for Israel will be answered (Romans 11:26 cf. Jeremiah 33:8; 50:20; Hosea 3:4-5).

2. Romans 15:30-33 – *Now I beseech you, brethren, for the Lord Jesus Christ's sake, and for the love of the Spirit, that ye **strive together with me in your prayers to God for me**; That I may be delivered from them that do not believe in Judaea; and that my service which I have for Jerusalem may be accepted of the saints; That I may come unto you with joy by the will of God,* *and may with you be refreshed. Now the God of peace be with you all. Amen.*

Prayer is work – *"that ye STRIVE together with me in your prayers to God for me…"* [Colossians 4:12, *"Epaphras, who is one of you, a servant of Christ, saluteth you, always LABOURING FERVANTLY for you in prayers…"*] To *strive* suggests a struggle as in an athletic event (1 Corinthians 9:25; 2 Timothy 2:5). When we pray, we are in a competitive mode. Prayer is often a battlefield/war-zone.[22]

---

[22] J. Sidlow Baxter describes how he learned to discipline himself to pray in *"The Battle Called Prayer"*—

My will was there to pray, buy my emotions were all facing the other way… My will and I stood face-to-face. I asked my will the straight question, "Will, are you ready for an hour of prayer?" Will answered, "Here am I, and I'm ready, if you are." So, Will and I linked our arms and turned to go for our prayer time. Suddenly all the emotions began pulling the other way and saying, "We're not coming!" I saw Will stagger just a bit, so I asked, "Can you stick with it, Will?" and Will replied, "Yes, if you can."

So Will and I went, and we got down to prayer, dragging those wriggling, obstreperous emotions with us. It was a struggle all the way through. At one point, when Will and I were in the middle of an earnest intercession, I found one of those traitorous emotions wandering away on the golf course, and it was all I could do to drag the rascal back. A bit later I found another of the emotions had slipped away two days ahead and was in the pulpit preaching a sermon I had not yet finished preparing!

Our praying must not be a casual experience that has no heart or earnestness. We should put as much fervor into our praying as an athlete puts into striving to win a competition.

William Cowper wrote, "Satan trembles when he sees the weakest saint upon his knees." It is not the weak believer he fears, nor the eloquence with which he prays—

At the end of that hour, if you had asked me, "Have you had a good time?" I would have had to answer, "No, it has been a wearying wrestle with contrary emotions and a truant imagination from beginning to end." What is more, that battle with the emotions continued for two or three weeks; and if you had asked me at the end of that period, "Have you had a good time in your daily praying?" I would have had to confess, "No, at times it has seemed as though the heavens were brass and God too distant to hear and the Lord Jesus strangely aloof, and prayer was accomplishing nothing."

Yet, something was happening. For one thing, Will and I really taught the emotions that we were independent of them. Also, one morning about two weeks after the contest began, just when Will and I were going for another time of prayer, I heard one of the emotions whisper to the others, "Come on you guys, it's no use wasting any more energy resisting… They'll just go on the same." That morning, for the first time, even though the emotions were still sullenly uncooperative, they were at least quiet, which allowed Will and me to get on with prayer undistractedly.

Then after another fortnight during one of our prayer times, when Will and I were no more thinking of the emotions than of the man in the moon, one of the most vigorous emotions unexpectedly sprang up and shouted, "Hallelujah!" at which all the other emotions exclaimed, "Amen! Praise the Lord!" And for the first time in the whole of James Sidlow Baxter— intellect, will, and emotions— were united in one coordinated prayer operation!

What he fears is the fact he is at the throne of grace appealing to his Heavenly Father to act on his behalf.

Three-fold prayer request

1) Deliverance from unbelievers. Paul asks prayer that he *"may be delivered from them that do not believe…"* Unbelievers are not sympathetic to those who seek to serve God.

> Football in the last decade has made the discovery that a position once taken for granted is one of the most important in the team. Salaries have risen and they are drafted in higher rounds… Offensive linemen. To watch a highlight is to see a QB throw, a receiver catch, a back score and rarely you focus on the lineman. But without his work the highlight would not happen. "Prayer warriors" are the offensive linemen that help make the work of a preacher effective in scoring a touchdown for "Team Jesus."

2) Paul asks that he *"may be accepted of the saints…"* Acceptance of the offering he was delivering to the church at Jerusalem

(cf. 1 Corinthians 1:11). They may reject it since it was a love offering from Gentiles.

3) That God would allow him to go to Rome to refresh them.

From reading the book of Acts, it appears Paul's prayer request was answered.

3. Ephesians 6:18-20 –*Praying always with all prayer and supplication in the Spirit, and watching thereunto with all perseverance and supplication for all saints; And for me, that utterance may be given unto me, that I may open my mouth boldly, to make known the mystery of the gospel, For which I am an ambassador in bonds: that therein I may speak boldly, as I ought to speak.*

Colossians 4:2-4 – *Continue in prayer, and watch in the same with thanksgiving; Withal praying also for us, that God would open unto us a door of utterance, to speak the mystery of Christ, for which I am also in bonds: That I may make it manifest, as I ought to speak.*

Both these prayer requests involve liberty in preaching the Gospel. Every minister, pastor, evangelist, and missionary needs people praying this prayer for them continually—"God, give our pastor and our missionaries, an OPEN DOOR to preach. Give them utterance to speak boldly as they ought to speak."

Paul was in prison when he wrote these words. Yet, Paul did not ask for the prison doors to be opened, but for preaching doors to be opened—"*...that God would open unto us a door of utterance, to speak the mystery of Christ… that I may make it manifest, as I ought to speak*" (see Ephesians 6:18-19; 2 Thessalonians 3:1).

- Pray for God to open doors of opportunity to witness to the unsaved (1 Corinthians 9:16; 2 Corinthians 2:12).
- Pray for God to remove obstacles that stand in the way of an unsaved person coming to Christ—Rebellious spirit; bitter attitude; intellectual pride.

<u>Example</u>: "Lord, I come in Jesus' name praying for John to be saved. I ask You to tear down the strongholds Satan has erected. I ask You to heal his spiritual blindness and open his eyes to the truth of the Gospel. Prepare John's heart to receive Your Word."

4. 2 Thessalonians 3:1-2 – *Finally, brethren, pray for us, that the word of the Lord may have free course, and be glorified, even as it is with you: And that we may be delivered from unreasonable and wicked men: for all men have not faith.*

This prayer is similar to the previous prayer requests we just studied. Paul's prayer request is primarily for the **prosperity** of God's Word. This was more important to Paul than his own personal protection in verse 2. There is nothing in Paul's requests about material or personal benefits, or the seeking of sympathy through the avenue of prayer requests.

Evangelist Tom Hayes writes: [23]

> It is a picture of an experienced and decorated soldier in the Lord's army humbly asking newly-inducted soldiers to assist him. Apparently, he had hit a snag in Corinth, and sensing his helplessness, desired them to pray that

---

[23] Tom Hayes, *Paths in 1&2 Thessalonians*, Saluda, North Carolina, 2003, p. 205.

the Word of God would have *"free course"* or "run well," and also *"be glorified,"* or "honored and esteemed." In his heart, he longed to see the ministry progress in Corinth as it had and did in Thessalonica.

Paul requests prayer that his audiences will listen to what he preaches without any interference or interruptions from politicians or religious leaders. ***"Free course"*** means without any obstruction or hinderance — It is a prayer for a speedy spread of God's Word. In the political and moral climate we live in today, this is something we should all be praying for. Amen!

How do your prayer requests line up to the prayer requests of Paul?

APPENDIX 1

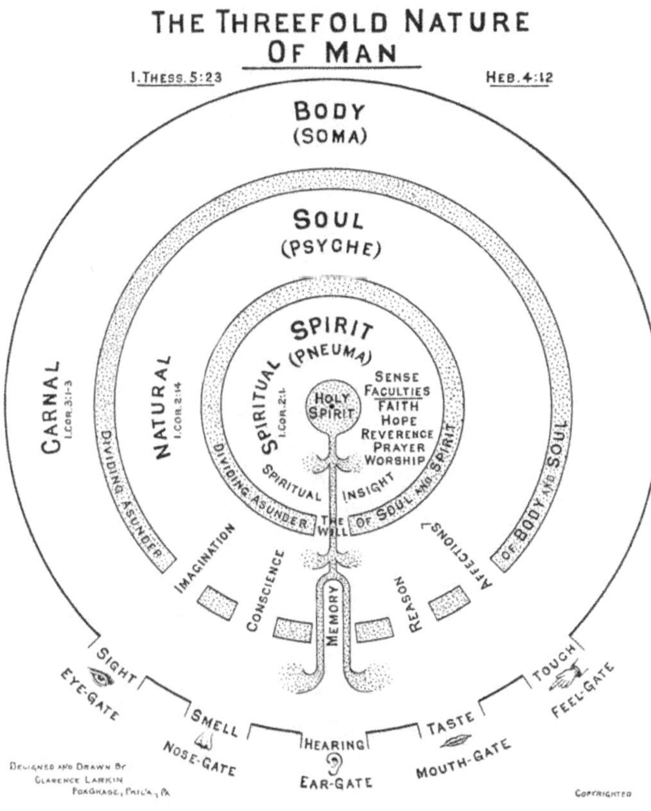

THE THREEFOLD NATURE OF MAN
I.THESS.5:23
HEB.4:12
BODY (SOMA)
SOUL (PSYCHE)
SPIRIT (PNEUMA)
CARNAL I.COR.3:1-3
NATURAL I.COR.2:14
SPIRITUAL I.COR.2:1
HOLY SPIRIT
SENSE FACULTIES
FAITH
HOPE
REVERENCE
PRAYER
WORSHIP
SPIRITUAL INSIGHT
DIVIDING ASUNDER
DIVIDING ASUNDER
OF SOUL AND SPIRIT
OF BODY AND SOUL
THE WILL
IMAGINATION
CONSCIENCE
MEMORY
REASON
AFFECTIONS
SIGHT
EYE-GATE
SMELL
NOSE-GATE
HEARING
EAR-GATE
TASTE
MOUTH-GATE
TOUCH
FEEL-GATE
DESIGNED AND DRAWN BY
CLARENCE LARKIN
FOXCHASE, PHIL'A, PA
COPYRIGHTED

Books by the Author

BOOKS:

BIBLE BELIEVER'S HANDBOOK OF CHURCH HISTORY (Vol. 1 – Foundations of Church History). Order from www.avhughes.com/store

SERMON OUTLINES ON PSALM 119 (spiral bound, limited quantities) [$10.95 plus postage - Order from www.avhughes.com/store] Also as version 2, available in Kindle or Paperback from Amazon.com.

WHAT WOMEN NEED [$9.95 plus postage]. Order from www.avhughes.com/store

INSIGHTS IN ISAIAH (A verse-by-verse study of the book of Isaiah). ***

WALKING WITH JESUS (67 outlined studies on the Life of Jesus Christ). ***

QUESTIONS JESUS ASKS (Messages of over 50 questions Jesus asked). ***

PEOPLE YOU CANNOT HELP ***

HIS NAME SHALL BE CALLED… (Names & Titles of Jesus). ***

THE CHRISTIAN HANDBOOK TO BIBLE INTERPRETATION (Tools of Bible Study). ***

DAVID: A Man After God's Heart (Over 70 studies of the Life of David). ***

KINGS and PROPHETS (Over 70 studies in 1 & 2 Kings and Chronicles). ***

JEWELS FROM JAMES (Studies in the book of James. 150 pages). Dispensational and practical lessons. ***

MOSES: The Man of God (Studies in Exodus, Numbers, Deuteronomy). ***

ROMANS (So Great Salvation). Exposition of the book of Romans with an emphasis of the doctrine of salvation. ***

ADVENTURES IN ACTS. Studies in the book of Acts. Dispensational and practical lessons about the early church. ***

***Available in Kindle or Paperback from Amazon.com.

COMING (in the works):

ECCLESIASTES (A natural man's view of life) Coming soon.

CONQUEST & COMPROMISE (Studies in Joshua and Judges. 250+ pages). Coming Summer, 2021

Beginnings (Studies in Genesis). Coming late summer, 2021

Points from Proverbs Coming in winter, 2021

Preaching in Psalms (Volume 1). Coming Spring 2022)

Shorter Epistles (Galatians, Ephesians, Philippians, Colossians). Practical doctrine. (2022 ?)

Five "T's" (1 & 2 Thessalonians; 1 & 2 Timothy; Titus). Church epistles (2022)?

Revelation. (2022 ?)